The Keys
to
High Level Production

Ken Unger
&
Tom Gau, CFP, CPA

Published by 5 Star Publications

First Edition 2003

Printed in the United States of America

ISBN 0-9742381-0-4

OTHER PRODUCTS BY
<u>MILLION DOLLAR PRODUCER INCLUDE:</u>

- *Membership to <u>www.MDPRODUCER.com</u>*
- *Complete Client Seminar Packages*
- *5 Star Performance Series Training Packages*
- *2-Day Financial Advisor Boot Camps*
- *Exclusive Coaching Programs*

These and other resources available at
<u>www.MDPRODUCER.com</u>.

Completed reading March 30, 2004

TRADEMARKED WORDS

NOT JUST WHAT TO DO, BUT <u>HOW</u> TO DO IT ™

DEDICATION

This book is dedicated to Ken Unger's mother,
Ethel Unger, who was his first teacher and educator.

It is also dedicated to Ken's family; his wife, Bonnie,
who is his life partner and has guided him to his success
in life, and his two daughters, Julia and Victoria, who are
the rays of sunshine in his very happy life.

This book is also dedicated to Tom Gau's three daughters,
Victoria, Angelica, and Sophia, who bring so much energy
and happiness into Tom's life, allowing him to maintain
his continuously positive outlook.

Finally, this book is dedicated to all those who have
helped Ken and Tom with their support, information,
and assistance. Without you, we would have never
learned the Keys to High Level Production. We wish
you continued success in all your endeavors.

- Ken Unger & Tom Gau -

Table of Contents

Introduction

As co-authors of this book and managing partners of Million
Dollar Producer, we wanted to take this opportunity to
introduce ourselves to you. It always seems much easier to take
advice from an expert, especially one who has worked in the
same situation you are in; therefore, let us take a minute to give
you the basics of our joint experience.

We have each been in the financial services arena for over 20
years. As partners and coaches, our experiences complement
each other. Tom has been a *Million Dollar Producer* for nearly
15 years. He started out the same way many of you started
your practices, but early on determined that in order to reach
his goal of financial independence he would have to work much
more efficiently than the way he'd been taught. For 2 weeks
each month, he still meets with 50-80 clients a week. The
strategies offered in this book are all ones that he continues to
use in his own highly successful practice. Ken has been a senior
executive since 1984. During this time span he was with a major
brokerage firm, a high-level broker/dealer, and a product
manufacturer. He is well respected industry-wide as a marketing
and efficiency expert. Since we joined forces in the year 2000,
we have been successfully coaching and offering advanced level
training for financial advisors with mid to very high production
levels.

During our tenures in the business, we have observed thousands of financial advisors, both successful and not so successful. In most cases, the unsuccessful advisors were not following certain practices that the successful advisors were. We labeled those certain practices the Ten Keys to Success.

We both believe strongly in the importance of learning from your mistakes, but wouldn't you agree that it is much easier and less costly if you can learn from other people's mistakes instead of your own? That is, in large part, what drove us to write this book. We developed a format that would share with you not only the most common mistakes many advisors have made, but also how to turn those mistakes around and get your practice on the road to success. Most importantly, we realize that theory is great, but often not very helpful. This book gives you step-by-step instructions on what you can do *right now* to move your practice to the next level.

As you know, the theory behind Million Dollar Producer is to share with you **not just what to do, but _how_ to do it!** All of these instructions and strategies have been tested and proven to work in Tom's own multi-million dollar practice!

We also need to take a moment to give credit where credit is due. Much of the research and content in this book comes from five main sources:

1. The over 20,000 financial advisors who have attended our 2-day training sessions (Boot Camps),

2. The high-level producers who have participated in our Exclusive Coaching Group,

3. The members of our website, www.mdproducer.com,

4. Our friends and colleagues, and

5. Tom and his unbelievably successful career as a leading producer.

Throughout this book you will find call-out boxes that refer to **_5 Star Tips._** These boxes are devoted to major ideas; suggestions or observations that have helped increase Tom's production significantly and/or maximized our time and efficiency. We understand how busy you are, but we also know first-hand the need to constantly review your business and your practices if you want to continue to improve. These boxes provide you with an easy way to review after you've read the book—whenever you have a few minutes to spare, simply flip through and read one of the call-out boxes to remind yourself of some key ideas and suggestions to bring your business up to the next level.

As we stated, at Million Dollar Producer, our goal is to teach financial professionals **not just _what_ to do to** improve their practices, **but _how_ to do it**, and that is exactly what we have tried to accomplish in this book. So . . . are you ready to honestly evaluate your practice? Are you open to new ideas for improving your current systems? If so, it's time to turn the page and begin your journey to success!

Key #1

Write a Business Plan

Perhaps the easiest mistake to make as a Financial Planner is to focus entirely on financial planning. Sounds crazy? It's not! You are in the financial planning business, and you need to run it like any business — with a formal, written business plan.

Unfortunately, many Financial Professionals do **not** focus on how to properly run their business, proceeding without any clear goals or plans for how to achieve those goals. Many other advisors were taught by these same professionals and entered the business focused solely on calling all the people they knew to get themselves started. They may have also felt that they didn't have the capital to properly establish a business and ended up simply "shooting from the hip." Unfortunately, once they did have the capital, it may have seemed easier to continue on with the same approach.

If you, like so many others, have fallen into the trap of working day-to-day without any long-term vision or written game plan, take a step back right now and ask yourself this question: If your company was listed on the New York Stock Exchange, would you recommend it to your clients as an investment?

All quality companies have established formal business plans in order to achieve their long-term goals, and so should you if you are going to have a successful practice.

Survey after survey identifies that one of the major problems that Financial Advisors have is they are so busy running their business they forget to sit down, take a look at the big picture, and plan their business.

When developing your plan, you need to have a sustainable, competitive – uniqueness, and you need to have strategic goals and tactical steps.

You need to have a reason why someone would find your shop attractive enough to do business. Additionally, you need to have two different types of direction for your practice: long-term strategic goals and short-term tactical steps.

Strategic goals are long-term decisions and they have an enormous impact on your practice. Tactical steps are your short-term steps, which are reversible. When implementing each tactical step, you need to continuously monitor your decisions so that they are in line with your strategic goals.

Market climates and responses will affect your tactical decisions and short-term goals, but should rarely change your long-term strategic decisions. Those long-term strategic goals are the ones that you need to revisit periodically, but not daily or weekly.

We did a survey of high-level producers and found that most of these advisors did not have a written business plan. They only had either:

- **A list of goals,**

- **A marketing plan, or**

- **A vision.**

In fact, here are samples of what some highly successful producers told us was the entire business plan of their branch.

- **"Our business plan is very simple — make money first."**

- **"We don't have time to put together a written business plan — we're too busy doing business."**

- **"We've been together so long that our business plan is we read each other's minds."**

When we asked why they didn't have a formal business plan, many said they didn't need one. We then asked if there were any areas they needed to improve and they said, absolutely. In fact, here is a list of the top areas they wanted to improve:

- **Communication**

- **Follow-up systems**

- **Operational efficiencies**

- **Prospecting**

- **Overall marketing strategy**

- **Shift to fee-based from commission-based, and**

- **Smooth coordinating of responsibilities**

They said their main challenges were:

- **Time management,**

- **Overall profitability,**

- **Managing staff and office,**

- **Compliance, and**

- **Keeping abreast of industry changes.**

Sitting down and taking time to write a business plan is no easy task, and we do not underestimate the time involved.

Most financial advisors tell their clients that people do not plan to fail, they just fail to plan. We all know the old saying "the cobbler's kids never have any shoes"; however, most of us understand the importance of helping our clients define their goals, needs, and objectives, and we know the odds of being successful and accomplishing these goals are significantly higher when they are written down.

Why? The main reason is writing it down holds you accountable.

How many times have we thought of an idea but forgot to write it down and never implemented this idea?

As an advisor, you need to write down your business plan!

Perhaps you are nodding your head as you read this, thinking, "OK, that sounds great, but how do I write a business plan?"

We have coached many financial planners like yourself in this crucial area, and we would like to share with you a simple, 8-step approach to developing a strong and functional business plan for your practice — one that will guide you to toward financial independence.

5 Star Tip

Do you spend all of your time working in your business and very little time working on your business?

Schedule time regularly to work on your business.

8 Steps to Developing a Functional Business Plan

STEP ONE: Determine who you are and what you have to offer.

Consider what you have to offer and who you can best help. Develop a clear, concise statement that describes your practice. This is your mission statement. Give it power. Take the time to choose verbs that bring life to your statement. (The time you take with this step will pay off, as you will see in **Key #3**, *Develop a Unique Selling Proposition*.)

STEP TWO: Write down your long and short-term goals.

These are your *strategic goals* — the core principles and strategies by which you will operate your practice. Make sure you list both monetary and non-monetary goals. It is not enough to have a goal of "doing well" or "improving my practice." If you are struggling to clarify your specific goals, try looking at other financial advisors you admire and describing what it is about their life and work that you wish you could duplicate. Consider also the following questions:

- Where you would like to be three years from now? Five years from now?

- How many assets would you like to have under management?

- How many days would you like to be working each month?

- What role do you see yourself playing in your practice today? How about in the future?

- What would you like to tell your grandchild of your greatest accomplishments?

5 Star Tip

When setting a goal for assets under management, you should consider a number of variables, including the time frame, inflation rates, and rates of return on your assets. It is also essential to determine whether you will be primarily commission-oriented or fee-based, or fee and commission.

Our Five Star Tip for setting this particular goal is to work backwards. For example, let's assume you would like $10,000 per month or $120,000 gross income before taxes from your practice. Let's also assume that you've prepared a budget for your business and anticipate your monthly expenses to be approximately $20,000 ($240,000 per year). If you pay out 90%, then your gross dealer concession needs to be approximately $400,000 per year. If we assume you charge a 1% fee on management investments, then you know you would need to set a goal of $40 million of assets under management to generate $400,000.

This form can help you determine how many new assets you need to bring in.

<u>Realistic Annual Production Goals</u>

A. My Annual Production Goal Is: $_____

B. My Current Fee or Residual Income Is: $_____

C. The New Production I Need Is: (A - B) $_____

D. My Average GDC from All Products & Programs: _____ %

E. Total New Assets I Need to Attract: (C / D) $_____

F. # of Weeks I Intend to Work this Year: _____

G. Amount of New Assets to Average a Week: (E / F) $_____

H. My Daily Goal Is: (G / 5) $_____

I. My Minimum Account Size Is: $_____

J. My Average Asset Size Is: $_____

K. Total New Accounts Needed Per Day: (H / J) _____

L. Total New Accounts Needed Per Week: (K x 5) _____

STEP THREE: Create a list of the steps you need to accomplish your goals.

These are going to primarily be *tactical steps* — the specific steps you decide are necessary to reach each of your goals. For example, if one of your long-term goals is to fully understand and service all the financial needs of people who are retired or about to retire, your tactical steps might include joining the AARP or becoming familiar with the new tax laws governing inherited IRAs.

STEP FOUR: Make a complete list of all the changes necessary to accomplish these goals.

You need to list the changes in your practice that are involved in achieving your goals. This list should be as thorough as possible!

STEP FIVE: Set a timetable.

What can you do *today* to start implementing your changes and steps that will help you realize your goals? What can you accomplish in one month? In one year? Prioritize your changes, then analyze each change and step that you've listed and give yourself a deadline for accomplishing them. This will help you back into a timeline for achieving your goals.

STEP SIX: Put the logic or rationale behind your assumptions into writing.

Include an annual revenue goal analysis and an annual budget. Please keep in mind that you need to be realistic. Try not to be overly aggressive or conservative. It is very hard to run a profitable business with unrealistic expectations.

For the revenue and expense side, you may want to try three quick scenarios; worst case, expected, and favorable case. If you do this, please try not to have too large a variance (no more than 15 – 25%).

STEP SEVEN: Develop a marketing plan.

All of these issues are discussed in more detail in further chapters, but a strong marketing plan is the nucleus of your business plan. The basics for developing a successful marketing plan are as follows:

- Identify your market niche. What kind of clients do you want to attract?

- List three (or more!) reasons why this particular type of client or prospect should do business with you instead of another firm.

- List specifically what services you will provide (including what resources you might need in order to be able to provide these services).

- Narrow down the field of marketing ideas. Which ones would be most successful in attracting and screening the prospective clients you are targeting? Don't be afraid to start multiple marketing projects at once (such as seminars, referral marketing, and direct mail), just be sure your plan is well organized.

- Don't forget your existing clients. Include a plan to strengthen your current relationships (perhaps by adding new services) so you can be more assured of keeping your clients and can approach them again for referrals.

- Set productivity goals with a focus on those areas you can control, such as how many client meetings you have each day or what you spend your time working on.

STEP EIGHT: Keep your business plan in view.

Once the hard work is done and your business plan is complete, don't shove it in your desk drawer and forget about it! Your business plan will be most effective if you periodically review it on a scheduled basis and make any and all necessary changes and updates.

Finally, when you are working on your business plan and figuring out your goals, don't be afraid to be aggressive. You should plan to significantly increase your assets under management each year. Do you realize that if you can accomplish a goal of a growth rate of 20% per year, your income will double about every four years?

"A 20% increase per year?" you are asking yourself. "Is this possible?"

Absolutely. But you must be willing to invest the time to write out a formal, functional business plan! If you are still not convinced of the importance of a business plan, just ask one of the thousands of our Boot Camp and coaching students who have accomplished a 20% growth rate by preparing a thorough and organized business plan and making use of the various marketing ideas and business systems we have designed, which are all available to **Million Dollar Producer** members on our website, **www.MDPRODUCER.com**

Key #2

Establish a Primary Niche

If you believe that the best financial planners are those who can be everything for everyone, think again! The most qualified and affluent clients and prospects (namely, the ones you are trying hardest to attract) want to deal with a specialist. If they need a heart transplant, they are going to demand the best heart surgeon available. Similarly, if they need help preparing their finances for retirement, they are going to seek out a retirement specialist, NOT someone who "specializes" in retirement, divorcees, college funding, inheritors, widows, teachers, etc.

Not only will clients and prospects not view you as a specialist, or expert, in their particular area if you spread yourself too thin, but you will end up losing money. For example, you will need to establish different marketing systems for each type of client you work with, resulting in both additional expenditure and reduced efficiency. It will also water down the effectiveness of your referrals if your existing clients don't see you as having any true specialty.

So what's the answer? The most successful financial advisors are those who have differentiated their practices by focusing on one particular market niche and becoming a specialist in that area. This is not as difficult as it may sound if you follow the four simple steps we have used with success with our coaching students.

STEP ONE: Choose the right niche.

How do you decide what is the right niche for you? The simplest way might be to work with what you already have — take your best clients, see what they have in common, and focus on trying to attract more clients like them. The common thread may be age, life style interests, gender or even occupation. But remember that you are looking for a segment of the population that is large enough so there are a reasonable number of candidates in your market area to prospect and work with.

Another approach would be to review your business plan. What is your mission statement? What did you determine that you have to offer? Who are you, and how are you different from your competition? What kind of clients would best be served with what you have to offer?

Finally, don't forget to review your bottom line! As you well know, there is a big difference between closing a $50,000 ticket and a $500,000 ticket; however, in most cases, the time it takes to close each one is approximately the same. Assuming you want to make more money, perhaps the most important factor in determining who you would like to focus your efforts on is finding a group of people who have a lot of money! Some of the market niches that currently have the highest concentration of wealthy Americans are small business owners, retirees, divorcees, widows and inheritors.

5 Star Tip

You must know your niche. People want specialists. You must be able to clearly communicate your specialty to clients. Most importantly, make sure the people in your niche have money to invest with you!

STEP TWO: Educate yourself.

Once you've chosen the niche that is right for you, one of the best ways to differentiate yourself from your competition is to make yourself into a specialist. Learn to think like your clients. Put yourself in their shoes. What are their hopes and fears? What are their needs and concerns? Educate yourself on their particular situation so you can customize your marketing presentations to specifically address their goals, needs and objectives. For example, if your market niche is retirees, then:

- Read books about topics of interest to retirees.
- Educate yourself about social security.
- Update yourself on tax laws pertaining to seniors (including the minimum distribution rules), or learn the rules regarding lump sum distributions.

- Learn how to become a retirement distribution specialist (by learning the complex new laws about inherited IRAs).
- Understand retirees' fear about losing their money.

★ ★ ★ ★ ★

5 Star Tip

Know everything you can about your niche. For example, wealthy people want protection from taxes and inflation more than anyone else.

Build trust by offering advice, not selling.

STEP THREE: Focus your practice on serving your niche.
Your goal here is to figure out how to best meet all the demands of your chosen market segment. Start by making three lists:

- all the products and services you currently provide
- all the products and services offered by your local competition
- all the products and services that would ideally be offered to best satisfy your niche (for example, if your niche is retirees, you might consider such services as estate planning or long-term care alternatives)

Using these lists you can put together a new menu of products and services for your practice that you can start offering on a regular basis.

And don't forget to review your office environment and client service approach to be sure they are best meeting the needs of your new market segment. For example, if your niche is retirees, make sure your seating is comfortable but not difficult to get out of. Review the periodicals available in your lobby to see if they are of interest to those in your niche. Retirees might be interested in certain periodicals or in informational publications like "The Top Ten Mistakes People Make When They Inherit an IRA" or "Is the Beneficiary of Your IRA the IRS?" (These publications are available on our website).

STEP FOUR: Market yourself to your chosen niche.

Once you've chosen your niche, educated yourself, and tailored your practice to meet the needs of that segment of the population, it's time to start aggressively marketing yourself and your practice.

Using what you've learned about your niche, start targeting prospects in your area. Where do the people in your target market congregate, and how can you make yourself available to as many prospects as possible? For example, if your niche is divorcees, think about giving seminars on "How to Manage Your Finances After a Divorce". If your niche is high-income earners or small business owners, perhaps you should network with realtors who specialize in selling expensive homes. If your niche is the retiree market, you could focus on retirement announcements in the newspaper; consider joining AARP, and offer seminars at senior centers where wealthy retirees gather.

More information about targeting your marketing to your chosen niche can be found in **Key #4**, *Create an Effective Marketing Plan*. Members can also access a great deal of specific information and helpful suggestions on our website.

Key #3

Develop a Unique Selling Proposition

You have a great prospect in the room right now who wants
to know exactly who you are and how you can help them.
Give yourself two minutes to answer their question. Ready?

Go!

OK, the test is over. Were you able to rattle off a clear, concise
word picture of yourself and your practice that drives home the
importance of your unique offerings? Don't feel bad if you
couldn't—most financial advisors can't do this. Their answers
tend to be either generic or unclear. In fact, one of the better
answers we get from our Exclusive Coaching Group members
is, "I'm honest and care about your finances and I help retirees
live comfortably." That's good, but will it generate a great
interest? Even a mild interest? Absolutely not!

★ ★ ★ ★ ★

5 Star Tip

You must continually ask yourself these questions:

Why should someone do business with me?

What makes me different?

How do I differentiate myself?

Every financial advisor needs a Unique Selling Proposition (USP) that sums up, quickly and clearly, those strengths that set them apart from the competition. You need to teach people, in one or two sentences, what you do best. If they don't know, or can't explain it clearly to others, how can you expect them to tell their friends what you do and get you referrals?

Unfortunately, many financial advisors never develop their USP and therefore fall into the abyss of being just another financial advisor pitching the same services or products. But developing a USP is not difficult, and developing a strong USP, while it takes a little more work, will greatly pay off!

Put simply, your USP must communicate to your prospects that you are aware of their problems and can solve them better than any of your competition!

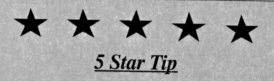

5 Star Tip

To best appeal to your niche, write down the top three concerns people in your niche have and incorporate this information into your Unique Selling Proposition (USP).

The easiest way to convince your target prospects to do business with you instead of someone else is to offer something *more than* or *different from* your competitors. Here are three steps that can help you develop your Unique Selling Proposition.

STEP ONE: Know your competition.

Have a friendly third party get on their mailing lists, review their marketing pieces and their ads, study what they offer, how they market, how they do business. Send a friendly third party into their offices for an interview to find out what they say and do. Ask clients who have been to other planners what they perceive as the differences between you and your competition.

STEP TWO: Emphasize whatever sets you apart.

Once you know your competitors' weaknesses and your own strengths, you can emphasize any significant differences, such as your credentials, years of experience, quality of work, service provided both before and after the sale, office hours, staff support, or whatever else sets you apart. And remember - don't be modest! Point out exactly why you are better than someone else. Your goal is to position yourself uniquely in your market and in your prospects' minds so that the only clear choice they have is to become your client.

STEP THREE: Don't forget to emphasize service and other bonuses.

Most financial products can be purchased from other planners at the same price. It is therefore extremely important to show that you take a personal interest in your clients and to emphasize the quality of your customer service. Offering freebies or bonuses to clients is another way to set yourself apart, even if these items cost you little or nothing, such as "free" periodic financial check-up meetings, "free" phone calls to answer questions or concerns, "free" short written financial plans, even free appointments with other professionals with whom you network. Go through what each of these things is worth in dollars so the prospect will appreciate their value. Even if your competition offers the same freebies, go through them anyway - your prospects most likely don't know these things are also offered elsewhere!

When you have completed these three steps, you should be able to concisely articulate the unique and attractive advantages that differentiate you from your competition. At this point we advise that you *put it in writing*. You can develop a fact sheet or brochure that lists each of the services you provide. (We use a brochure called "Gold Medal Service," which is available to use as a guide for members of our website.) Use this brochure in your office by going through the list and asking prospects whether other advisors also offer the same services you do. Most importantly, let them take it home and have it as a reference, so they can review it on their own time and really appreciate everything you have to offer them.

Key #4

Create an Effective Marketing Plan

What is your system for generating a healthy number of leads on a regular basis? Unfortunately, most advisors do not have a formal and disciplined marketing system - they either hope for some referrals, make cold calls or contact friends. In fact, many advisors who *had* successful practices found them withering after awhile for lack of a good system to generate additional business. The old saying is true - if your business isn't growing, it's dying.

Many financial planners confuse sales and marketing, thinking these are one and the same. **The purpose of marketing is to get qualified people in front of you.** The purpose of sales is to transact business. Now you grasp the true importance of marketing - after all, you can't transact any business if you don't have anyone to talk to!

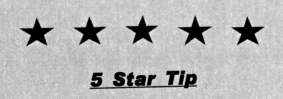

★ ★ ★ ★ ★

5 Star Tip

Marketing needs to be done 12 months a year; you must avoid the "feast or famine" syndrome.

If you're going through this book in order, then you already have a good head start on your marketing plan. You already targeted a particular audience, which is your primary niche. You already educated yourself about the problems and concerns of those in your niche. And in developing your USP, you defined yourself as someone who knows those problems and can solve them better than anyone else. This will be the core of your marketing - you need to sell the *solution*, not the product.

Our website offers members an enormous quantity of information, tips and resources for marketing your practice. The following are a few of the key steps to developing a successful marketing plan:

STEP ONE: Target your marketing.
Determining your market niche and developing your USP allows you to now market directly to the people most qualified to become highly profitable clients. Paint a bull's-eye on the exact segment of the population you want as clients, and aim your arrow there!

5 Star Tip

If you want to be successful at anything, you must have three things:

1. The desire to do something, and enjoy doing it;

2. The expertise to do it; and

3. The time to do it.

STEP TWO: Include a call to action.

Direct marketing should *always* contain a call to action. You need to specifically ask people to contact your office, attend a seminar, obtain information from you or make an appointment. Once you get their name and address you can add them to your computer database for future marketing, allowing you to eventually rely less on newspaper ads and other more expensive forms of marketing. Accumulate as large a database of qualified leads as possible. Just because they aren't ready to be closed now doesn't mean they won't be ready in the future!

STEP THREE: Use a two-pronged approach—emotion and logic.

Don't fall into the trap of assuming that high-net-worth prospects are more sophisticated than the rest of the population. Their financial situations may be more sophisticated, but as people they are no different from anyone else. People only *need* food, water, clothing and shelter. All other purchases are based on *want*, and these purchase decisions are therefore usually based on emotion. Yet at the same time, people will seek out logical reasons to support their emotional decisions. Therefore, your initial marketing approach should be to arouse strong emotions (fear, hatred of paying taxes/IRS, greed, love) to shake them up, unsettle them and get them emotionally involved. After that, marketing needs to provide specific information and facts that appeal to the logical mind and, if possible, clear away any logical objections.

★ ★ ★ ★ ★
5 Star Tip

Marketing must accomplish 2 things;

appeal to the client's emotions and show your ability

to solve that client's needs.

Remember: emotional reasons usually outweigh

economic ones in the decision making process.

STEP FOUR: Don't be afraid of long copy.

The traditional idea of marketing materials dictates that short and to the point is the only way to go. However, the more complex and costly a decision a person is making, the more information they require, and the only way to provide a lot of specific information is through a lot of text. For many financial products, long copy works much better in bringing people to the point of a close. Long, however, does not mean boring. Make your approach as interesting, informative and emotionally exciting as possible. And conclude by asking for the order! This is the most powerful call to action there is - don't hesitate to use it.

STEP FIVE: Diversify your marketing approaches.

You tell your clients to diversify their investments, and you should use the same approach to your marketing campaign.

1. *Diversify the media that you use.*

   Marketing comes in many varieties, including public seminars, speaking engagements at private organizations or clubs, direct mail, advertising, networking with CPAs and attorneys, and referrals from clients. (Our website contains detailed, step-by-step instructions and advice for getting started in any of these approaches.) If you use only one approach, its returns will begin to decline. If you use several approaches, however, you will find that they confirm your credibility in the public's mind and reinforce their need to take action. Using two forms of marketing will often triple, not double, your response. Fliers and other targeted direct mail, when added to a minimum of newspaper ads, tends to be the most cost-effective way to generate more highly qualified leads than you can handle.

2. *Diversify the product or service you are marketing.*

   For example, during March and April you might want to emphasize tax planning. Around the year-end holidays you might want to emphasize estate planning. Or you may want to focus on tax-free investing one month and growth investments the next. It doesn't matter which particular "hook" lands them in your office; once you have them in your database, you then have the opportunity to sell them on all the products and services you offer. This approach is called "up-selling."

STEP SIX: Test the effectiveness of each approach.

Don't assume that a certain piece or approach will work just because you understand your market niche, your USP and your clients' "hot buttons." Test the bottom-line results on a small scale before spending much money. Also, don't forget to periodically test your *existing* marketing material to see what's working and what isn't. So how do you go about testing a marketing approach?

1. Test in a way that allows you to track and quantify results.

2. Place your ad enough times or send out enough mail pieces to get a true test result.

3. Don't be too quick to throw something away if it doesn't work the first time. There could be a lot of factors that contribute to a first-time failure, such as the timing or manner of distribution. Also, consider that maybe only one or two aspects need to be changed rather than the whole thing being thrown away.

★ ★ ★ ★ ★
5 Star Tip

Marketing must always have an emotional appeal and should talk about things that bother clients and prospects.

Always think about mentioning taxes in your advertising. It is a prospect and client hot button.

You know how important marketing is. You know that to really increase your profits, you must increase not only the number but also the quality of the prospects you meet with, and attracting more quality prospects is the key role of effective marketing. But the question still remains - are you acting in accordance with this knowledge? Are you allowing at least 10-20% of your gross revenues to go back into marketing in order to generate additional leads for your practice? Are you blocking off time on your calendar each day for marketing? If you're not, chances are that meetings, administrative burdens or other tasks are filling up whatever time you might have mentally set aside, and your marketing - along with the growth of your practice! - will suffer. We will cover this topic in more detail in **Key #10**, *Delegate Everything that can be Delegated!*

Don't let money stop you from marketing. Marketing doesn't have to be expensive if you use your dollars wisely. By making small, significant changes to your current marketing techniques, or by adding new techniques at little or no cost, you can dramatically increase your results. For example, simply rewriting the headline of an ad you are currently using, or adding in an offer for a free consultation, can bring in a much greater number of leads at no additional cost over what you were already spending.

But perhaps you are not currently advertising because you don't feel that you can afford to spend *any* money. If that is the case, you need to change your perspective. Instead of focusing on what your marketing costs, start thinking in terms of what it yields! If you spend $1000 that you **know** will generate at least $10,000, what is your **net** cost? Can you afford **not** to spend that money?

★ ★ ★ ★ ★

5 Star Tip

You need to view marketing not as an <u>*expense*</u>*, but as an* <u>*investment*</u>*.*

Expenses don't yield returns; marketing does!

Key #5

Become a Specialist

5 Star Tip

You want people to look at you as their financial doctor; therefore you must always try to act as a doctor would.

We have already addressed the idea of becoming a specialist in **Key #2**, *Establish a Primary Niche*. You have already targeted a certain segment of the population to deal with in your practice, and you have seen how this can help focus your marketing resources. Unfortunately, many advisors are still tempted to take on any type of client. You must resist temptation and learn when to say "No"!

5 Star Tip

Stay focused. Try not to do anything that is not going to apply to your niche.

Taking on a client outside of your primary niche will cause many inefficiencies. For example, let's say a small business owner walks in your door. This looks like a very tempting prospect. However, if you have put your time and effort into educating yourself on every aspect of assisting a retiree, not only is all that information going to be wasted on this new client, but he will most likely ask you to do things for him that you don't normally do for retirees, and possibly things you have never done before. Now consider the time and money it will take to properly service this client. Also, you will lose your status as a specialist and may not do as good a job for this new client since you haven't prepared yourself for dealing with his particular situation.

Think of a major company, such as General Motors. If GM did research and found there was a demand for a new automobile, but it was so unique that only 100 people would purchase this car, would GM go through the time and trouble to create such a vehicle? No, and neither should you! If you do not perform an activity or provide a service on a regular basis, it will cost you too much time and money to do it for a very small number of clients.

Never sell or do anything unless you are going to do a lot of it! You can't do everything for everyone, and you can't be an expert in everything. By being highly selective regarding your niche and activities, you will become a specialist in your field and will be granted more respect because of your area of expertise.

Key # 6

Maintain a Contact Management System

How often do you meet with your clients? Many advisors have told us that they only meet with their clients annually. If all you are doing is selling them one product or service, such as life insurance, then this might be enough. However, if your goal is to truly be their comprehensive financial advisor, then you will usually need to meet more often than this in order to retain a good relationship with your client and get the referrals that you deserve from them.

In fact, most advisors don't realize how important the relationship is to the client. Clients want communication. They want to feel that you are thinking about them even when they are not sitting in your office. Clients are likely to leave their advisors if they only meet with them once a year and/or they feel like they are being ignored. Therefore, it is *essential* to keep in close contact with your clients (even if you are not selling them anything), because if you don't, chances are they won't even be around when it is the appropriate time to recommend a change for them.

5 Star Tip

Code everyone in your database. Either they are clients and they must be coded "A", "B", or "C", or code them as prospects.

"A" clients must be met with quarterly.

"B" clients must be met with every six months.

"C" clients should be met with when necessary.

Keep in mind that it costs much less to keep a client than to get a new one. If you want to improve your relationship with your clients and increase your client retention rate and the quality of your referrals, start by following these simple steps!

STEP ONE: Develop a contact management system.

Input all your clients and prospects and their information into a client management database. (Since prospects may not be ready to make a purchase the first time they meet with you, you should keep them in your database with an eye toward future sales unless they are completely unqualified.) This will allow you to keep track of who you have met with and when. The database should also be able to sort your clients by size, importance, centers of influence, and a range of other areas.

5 Star Tip

You need to establish a client factory. The first meeting is the raw material, where you learn about the client. The second stage is the work in progress, where you prepare a plan or a report. The third stage is a closing meeting, which is the finished product. You need to plan a sufficient number of all three stages for the "factory" not to stop production. Client service meetings are in addition to these three stages.

To be at your best you need to set goals. Also, keep a tracking system for how many appointments you have of each type.

STEP TWO: Determine how often you need to meet with your clients.

In order to maintain a good relationship, you should meet with your top clients at least quarterly and your other clients at least semi-annually. If you decide that you do not want to meet with them as often as that, then it is very likely that they will be with another advisor in the future!

STEP THREE: Consider the benefits of follow-up meetings.

Why meet with a client again after you've recently made a sale? There are quite a number of benefits to doing this:

- Reduces any buyer's remorse your client may have.

- Gives you the opportunity to deal with any problems, which otherwise might have grown bigger and bigger with time.

- Helps reduce your long-term liability exposure in case something goes wrong with their investment, since clients are much less likely to sue someone who has shown genuine interest in them.

- Provides an excellent opportunity to make additional sales, solicit referrals and continue to strengthen your relationship.

- Allows you a chance to keep your client educated about all the products and services you offer. You don't want them going to someone else for something that you are able to do for them.

- Allows you a chance to educate the client about their own needs for your products and services.

STEP FOUR: Continuously and repeatedly market to your database.

After you accumulate a significant computer database of highly qualified prospects, as well as existing clients who are prospects for future sales, make sure that each name in your database receives some form of marketing from you periodically. Don't make the mistake of considering marketing to existing clients to be a waste of money. Quite the opposite, it may be even more important to your existing clients than to your prospects. Remember, these people have already said yes to you, and continuing to stay in touch with them is inexpensive and generates almost pure profit. The more you are in contact with your clients, the more you show them your concern for their wants and needs, and the less they will feel they are not being properly serviced and need to turn elsewhere.

Always Review a Client's Total Picture

Here is a fact that should startle you—it is estimated that the average financial advisor is only aware of one-third of their clients' assets. One-third! And yet it's easy to see how this can happen if advisors are transaction oriented. By focusing only on certain aspects of a client's situation they never get the total picture. And without the total picture, they can never have all the information they need to make the appropriate recommendations for their clients.

Do you want to be a salesman of financial products, or do you want to be a financial doctor, guiding your client to financial health and strength? We can help you move from being good at what you do to being at the highest and most respected levels of this profession by following a few key steps:

STEP ONE: Start reviewing all five areas of each client's financial picture at the Initial Client Interview.
These are:

   A. Protection

   B. Estate Planning

   C. Retirement Planning

D. Income Tax Planning

E. Investments

This is critical for two reasons. First, not many advisors do this, so it will make you stand out from your competition. Second, and most importantly, focusing only on investments and ignoring the other areas means ignoring sales opportunities and the chance to start a comprehensive financial relationship with your clients.

★ ★ ★ ★ ★

5 Star Tip

Always explain to prospects and clients that you can best help them if you do three things:

1)   gather data,

2)   analyze that data, and

3)   only then can you make educated recommendations.

Get prospects to bring several things with them to the first meeting, including their pension details, tax returns and all of their most recent investment statements.

You cannot give proper advice without all the facts.

Our website offers members a handy reference to use during initial client interviews—a Checklist for Financial Planning, which provides all the information necessary for covering these areas in a brief outline format.

STEP TWO: Understand the interconnectedness of the five areas. While we have separated these areas out, you still have to keep in mind that they are all part of a whole, and each one can impact the others. For example, if you can help reduce the client's taxes, this will help them invest more, which in turn will help them retire earlier. Another way to look at it is that if they invest properly, you can reduce their taxes, which again will help their income during retirement. However, if they do not hold title of their investments properly, they may need additional insurance for protection against estate taxes! You can see how if you only address one area, it would be easy to make a poor recommendation. Not only is this not the best thing for a client, but it also leaves you open to losing your clients to competitors who *will* review their other needs.

5 Star Tip

Show an interest in the total financial picture and you will become your client's financial doctor. Always ask probing questions such as:

"Do you have a will?

A living trust?

When were they updated?

If you like, I can set you up a review with an attorney after our next interview."

Let's go back to the idea of being a financial doctor for a minute. Now, if you went to a doctor with a pain in your arm, the doctor would not only look at your arm, but would also look at other parts of your body, because it could be that your heart, for example, could be the cause of the pain in your arm! Just as the various parts of your body work together, separate but connected, so do the various parts of your financial picture. Therefore, to address a client's total financial picture, you must give your client a "financial physical" and review everything before making your recommendations.

STEP THREE: Realize the benefits of the additional time expenditure.

Yes, it does take more time to review all five areas with a client. In fact, the last three areas (retirement planning, income taxes, and investments) usually require the most time, but are also often the areas clients are the most interested in. Once a client's estate planning needs and insurance issues are finally completed, they tend to remain fairly constant. However, the last three areas are more dynamic, as investments constantly go up and down, income tax laws change almost every year and people's cash flow needs also vary year to year. But as we mentioned before, this is time well spent, and will help you keep more of your current clients, draw in new clients, and will also help you make better recommendations for your clients.

★ ★ ★ ★ ★
5 Star Tip

When meeting with prospects, prioritize the top three problems that prospect has and deal with these first. If your prospect is not open to working on the weakest area of their plan, then you are less likely to convert that prospect to a client.

Key #8

Establish a Minimum Investment Amount

You are a professional. Have you ever given serious thought to what your time is worth? Most advisors will agree that their time is worth *at least* $100 per hour. Unfortunately, many advisors will take on a client with whom they make significantly less than this amount! In **Key #5**, *Become a Specialist,* we tried to emphasize the importance of selecting your clients carefully and not taking each and every person who comes through the door. Wouldn't you agree that you are doing a disservice to both yourself and your clients if you do not make enough money to stay in business?

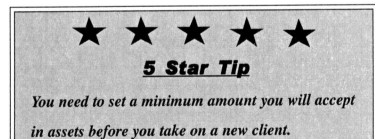

★ ★ ★ ★ ★

5 Star Tip

You need to set a minimum amount you will accept in assets before you take on a new client.

For example, let us assume that a new client approaches an advisor wanting to establish a relationship by opening up an IRA account in the amount of $2,000. If this is a commissionable product, and the commission is 5%, then the advisor would earn $100 on this transaction (assuming your payout is 100%).

However, don't you think it would take that advisor well over an hour to meet with the client; gather all of the critical information regarding the client's financial situation; find out the client's goals, needs, and objectives; fill out the paperwork; mail the proper confirmations to the client and assist the client over the next few years regarding his account? If you want to succeed you must work smarter, not harder. Stop taking on small clients who demand too much of your time for too little commission.

STEP ONE: Determine how much time you require to perform various services.

For example, let's say you find it is taking you at least a few hours to meet with a client and gather their data. Then you add in the estimated time you will have to spend meeting with the client over the next few years and arrive at a total of 10 hours.

STEP TWO: Determine your minimum investment amount.

Take your figure from step one (we'll use 10 hours) and multiply it by the amount you think your time is worth. In our example, 10 hours at $100 per hour is $1,000. If you are earning a 4% commission on a transaction, this means that the minimum amount you need clients to invest would be $25,000.

STEP THREE: Identify which clients are essential to your practice.

A deeper understanding of your clients will help you in your search for new, *highly qualified* clients. You may know which clients bring in the most revenue (your A list), but do you understand clearly *who they are* in terms of the characteristics they have in common? Ask yourself why they choose to do business with you. Ask them, the next time you meet with them, "Mr. /Mrs. Client, if you were to sit down with a neighbor, friend, or colleague who is in a financial position similar to your own and describe my relationship with you and what services I provide, how would you do that?" The answer may shock you, but it is very important that you understand your clients' perceptions of you and your services.

One of our most successful coaching group participants tried this with his clients and the first couple of clients came back and said "That's easy, you are our retirement guy", and "I would describe you as someone who looks at my retirement plan to make sure I can retire on time." What this helped our coaching student find out is most of his clients only recognized him for *a portion* of what he did, therefore they couldn't properly explain to friends or colleagues that he offered full and comprehensive financial planning services. After learning this, he was able to increase his business by more than 30% over the next six months by calling in all of his A and B clients and reviewing with them what services he did offer and how he wanted them to think of him.

STEP FOUR: Overcome your hesitation to upgrade your practice.

Many advisors think about upgrading but are afraid they will end up losing money if they start turning clients away. This is not the case! By selecting only the more qualified clients, you will earn more money by working the same number of hours or even less! Also, consider the timing. At the time we are writing this book, there are so many investors who are nervous and/or unhappy with their current financial situations, we use that as an opportunity to capture a considerable amount of new business! As we always tell our exclusive coaching group, vision creates opportunity, and a confused investing public gives you the chance to step in and address their confusion. By putting in just a little bit of extra effort now, you can dramatically expand your business.

STEP FIVE: Figure out how to be exceptional.

Don't rely on what *you think* is valuable to your clients—it is the job of financial advisors today to *find out exactly* what their clients value most and which of those valued services they can deliver as well as (or better than!) anyone else in their marketplace. That knowledge will revolutionize your practice. It can be the switch that, once pushed, can set in motion instant growth. This is because a clear and specific customer driven focus effectively communicated to everyone in your organization will provide direction. And the best part is, if you've developed your Unique Selling Proposition, this step is probably already done!

STEP SIX: Modify your practice to create a value-driven strategy for your clients.

Look at the area of convergence between the things that you do best and the things your most profitable clients value most. Then develop a laser-like focus that allows you to create a value-driven strategy for all your clients.

- If you are currently providing a service that is not something you do well *and* your clients don't value it, seriously consider cutting back or stopping it altogether.

- If you are providing a service that you do well but your clients don't value, is it worthwhile to provide it? You might be better off spending your time and energy improving the services your clients do value instead.

- If there is something that your clients value very much, but it is not something that you do well, consider outsourcing. For example, if your clients are very concerned about coordinating their investments with their tax situation and you are not comfortable with reviewing tax forms (not preparing but reviewing), you could partner with an accounting firm that could help you provide that service, or you could build that capability internally.

- When you find those services you offer that your clients value most *and* you have strong capabilities in, this is where you need to build that laser-beam focus. This is your point of attack. This will allow you to create a unique value strategy you can sell to your prospects and clients. This is where you can really market yourself for new business both within your existing book of business and in your community in general.

STEP SEVEN: Draw attention to yourself.

Whatever your marketing campaign is, please consider reviewing it and even adding to it with the goal of attracting more clients who meet your new minimum investment amount. Use your marketing plan to target qualified prospects and define for them what specific values they can expect your organization to deliver in a high quality way each and every time. Put together a strong package that differentiates you from all others. Start a massive referral campaign, asking everyone you do business with (who meets your minimum account size). Commit to a regular seminar campaign, if you haven't already. (Even in a volatile environment, attendance may be down a bit but your closing ratio should remain strong.) Focus your whole practice on communicating clearly to existing clients and the community as a whole what services you provide and why they should do business with you.

Key #9

Meet Regularly with Qualified Leads

You agree that it makes sense to concentrate on your revenue-producing activities if you want to make more money, right? Well, you make the most money when you are meeting with clients! Simply being *busy* (putting out fires, doing administrative tasks, etc.) won't grow your business—you must be productive with your time and continually meet with clients.

★ ★ ★ ★ ★

5 Star Tip

There are only two rules to being successful in this industry:

#1 Always be meeting with clients.

#2 Always remember rule #1!

You must be able to establish a system to meet with enough clients in order to justify your practice and your increasing expenses. There are a number of steps you can take in order to generate enough appointments with qualified leads:

STEP ONE: Make prospecting and marketing a priority.

Without them, you won't have nearly as many client meetings, so it's important to realize that prospecting and marketing are on the same priority level as a client meeting. You should block off time in your calendar for prospecting and marketing (at least one hour each day), creating a daily marketing regimen. It is very easy to procrastinate or get sidetracked by taking a long distance call from a friend during this period of time, but would you do that if you were in front of a client?

Marketing and prospecting can be much like going to the health club. You know it is good for you and will produce predictable results, but it is not something that you enjoy and therefore you avoid it whenever possible by claiming you have more important things to do. Like exercising, marketing and prospecting are easier to do if you have an established daily routine.

STEP TWO: Enlist the help of your staff.

Explain to your staff that you expect them to view your marketing hour as they would if you were in with a client. Instruct them on what calls you will take during that hour and what calls you will not.

★ ★ ★ ★ ★
5 Star Tip

The Number One function of a sales assistant is to keep your calendar filled with appointments. Getting you in front of people is their most important job. Communicate this expectation to staff.

STEP THREE: Make as many calls as possible.

You may be tempted to talk longer so that you'll have to make fewer calls during your allotted hour. Obviously, this is counter-productive! Make your calls as brief as possible, keeping in mind that the purpose of the call is *to set up an appointment,* not to sell a product or service. If necessary, keep an egg timer in front of you to time your calls. You should only use 3 minutes to make that appointment.

STEP FOUR: Consider calling during off-peak hours.

Many people are the busiest from 9 to 5. If you are calling someone at home, you might try to reach them from 6:30 to 8:00 pm. If you are calling someone at work, try calling between 8:00 and 9:00 am or during the lunch hour. Many decision-makers work during these off-peak hours in order to get more accomplished. Also, their secretaries are often *not* working during these times; making it easier for you to reach the person you are looking for.

STEP FIVE: Keep the client file or database in front of you.

This will allow you to take better notes during your calls or leave yourself a reminder note on your action-pending list on your computer if the client tells you to call back at a later date. You don't want anything to fall through the cracks! When you do call the client back, remind them that you're calling when they asked you to. This will help you get a foot in the door.

STEP SIX: Avoid playing phone tag.

If you have to leave a message, inform the person of the best time to call you back. You might even let them know that the purpose of the call is to set up a meeting. That way, they might be able to simply set up the appointment with your administrative assistant when they call back.

5 Star Tip

For important clients you are trying to reach, tell the client to let your office know that when they call you back, please have your staff interrupt you even if you are in a meeting. This way you will not continually play phone tag with key people.

STEP SEVEN: Tape record yourself.

Listen to your own phone conversations and see how you sound. Try changing either the tone of your voice or the way you come across until you sound just the way you want to. Practice makes perfect! (These tapes can also help you train other people, such as sales assistants or secretaries. Let them learn from you so they can do it your way!)

5 Star Tip

Set a time limit for all client meetings and communicate that limit to the client.
If necessary, have your assistant call to interrupt so the meeting can be kept within the limit.

STEP EIGHT: Purchase a small mirror and put it on your desk.

By doing this, you can see your own expressions (good or bad!) and see how you look in front of clients and how you might be communicating while you are on the phone. For example, try smiling more when you are talking with someone and you'll notice how your attitude and results will change dramatically!

Key #10

Delegate Everything That Can Be Delegated!

In **Key #9**, *Meet Regularly with Qualified Leads*, we talked about the importance of focusing on revenue-producing activities (client meetings and generating client meetings). To do this, however, you must be willing to make changes in order to make the most effective use of your time!

As we mentioned in **Key #8**, *Establish a Minimum Investment Amount*, your time should be worth at least $100 per hour. Think about what activities you currently do that you could pay someone else much less than $100 an hour to do for you, such as:

- Filing
- Copying
- Confirmations
- Filling out client applications
- Making appointments

Only you can give advice to your clients, but there are many other things you do every day which could easily be delegated to someone else. How do you determine which things to delegate and how to go about it? Below are several steps to get you started:

STEP ONE: Keep a time sheet for one week.

List specifically, in 15-minute increments, what you are doing each day for a week. At the end of the week, most advisors will realize that they have spent less than one-third of their time doing what they should be doing — meeting with clients.

5 Star Tip

Keep a precise time sheet for one full week. You make money by being in front of clients, not by doing filing. Every time you are doing something other than being in front of a client, ask yourself if you could have been doing something more effective (like speaking with a client on the phone).

STEP TWO: Have a member of your staff observe you.

During those times when you are not meeting with clients or working on prospecting/marketing, have someone in your office observe the specific things you do and write down those tasks they feel they could be trained to do for you.

STEP THREE: Systematize!

One of the key secrets of a top producer is to systematize as much as possible! Once you create a detailed, written procedure for a particular task, it is much easier to delegate to someone else.

STEP FOUR: Hire a good staff.

If you are going to delegate, you must have a good staff that you trust. But perhaps you don't currently have a staff and think you can't afford to hire help. The truth is, you can't afford not to! Remember when you figured that your time is worth $100/hour? Is that really how much you want to pay yourself for filing, filling out paperwork, etc.? You can pay someone else much, much less than this to do those kinds of things, leaving yourself free to focus on revenue-generating activities.

Whether you share an assistant, hire someone part-time or staff an entire office with help, it is important to find the right people. Besides putting an ad in the paper, you might try asking your broker/dealer or other broker/dealers in your area if they have any prospects (yes, talk to the receptionist, who usually knows everything!), asking your local bank or trust department, asking existing staff if they know any qualified candidates, or placing an ad in the FPA newsletters or bulletins.

College interns also provide an inexpensive source of assistants. Although their services won't be at the highest level, they generally work hard and may come to work for you after graduation (already fully trained by you, of course!). And don't overlook the obvious - you don't need to hire another person if your current staff feels they can take on more work.

Once you have a candidate, you can determine how suitable they are by asking the right questions:

- What experience do they have in processing securities applications?

- What experience do they have in processing life insurance or annuity applications?

- How many years' experience have they had in the financial planning industry?

- What college education or degrees do they have?

- Has the applicant completed a Financial Para planner Course?

- Has the applicant had any sales experience?

- Has the applicant lived in the area very long? (good for referrals)

- Does the applicant have any security or insurance licenses?

- Is the applicant more of a processor or a sales person?

Obviously, you must also carefully review the basics such as previous job longevity, word processing skills, computer literacy, whether they have their own transportation (if you need them to deliver packages or perform other customer service items), professional appearance and telephone voice, and letters of recommendation.

5 Star Tip

Pay an assistant $10 an hour so you can earn $100 an hour.

STEP FIVE: *Do not* delegate training.

Although it means time away from clients, and there is always a possibility that this new employee will not work out, it is imperative to look at training as an investment in your future. Take the time to train them to accomplish various tasks to your standards and expectations. Try to walk the fine line between being very clear about exactly how you operate your business and how you like to work, and also being open to any suggestions or ideas this new person may have. You are paying for their experience — make use of it! Also, set a good example. An assistant will not put in 100% if they do not see you putting in 100%. Define your specific goals and prioritize the things they must do to help you with those goals. Put your expectations in writing in their job description, check in with them on a regular basis, and don't be afraid to make changes if you feel you've gotten off track.

Many financial planners hit a stumbling block when it comes to training; namely, they believe they can do the tasks better and more quickly than their assistant, or that it will take more time to train them than it's worth. If you find yourself feeling this way, you need to set these beliefs aside! Try training them to do these things one at a time. Allow yourself to become comfortable with the way they are performing the first task you delegate before you move on to the next one. This way you won't overwhelm them and you won't be a nervous wreck thinking the things you've delegated are not being handled the way you want them to be.

STEP SIX: Train your assistants to save you time.
Here are several things your assistant should be doing for you so you can focus on more important things:

- *Phone messages.* Ask them to find out the specific reason for the call and the best time for you to return the call. Telephone tag is a huge waste of time. In addition, if a client calls, have the receptionist look in your database to see when the client last had a meeting. It could be time to schedule another appointment rather than just returning a phone call!

- *Setting appointments.* Give them the minimum number that you expect them to book, and teach them how to overcome objections and get people into your office. (Our website provides members with Sample Phone Scripts to use in training assistants in this area.)

- *Confirming appointments.* Make sure that appointments are confirmed with both a reminder card and a telephone call. Isn't that what your doctor does?

- ***Customer service.*** Make sure your assistant knows who your A, B and C clients are so they can give the A clients greater attention.

- ***Signatures.*** Instruct them to leave all paperwork requiring your signature in your In Box, and then return them once signed.

- ***Mail.*** Inform them as to which items you will want to see and which to file, throw away or delegate to others. Teach them to screen all mutual fund statements to look for redemptions or purchases not logged by your firm so you can review those files.

- ***Questions and issues for discussion.*** Request your assistant to save these, if possible, for one weekly staff meeting to avoid a barrage of daily interruptions. (One weekly rep meeting is also a good idea.)

5 Star Tip

Keep a prioritized To–Do list.

Also have your assistants keep To–Do lists and report to you once a week regarding their lists and what is still outstanding.

STEP SEVEN: Delegate paperwork.

Do important paperwork that requires an immediate response, delay any items that can wait, and delegate everything else. Once clients have accepted your recommendations, introduce them to the member of your staff who will help them fill out the applications. Reassure them that they are not being passed off to a junior rep. Explain that you alone are their financial advisor, and while you never delegate advice and you will always be available to answer their questions, you do delegate the paperwork. Clients will understand this and accept it.

STEP EIGHT: Delegate operational customer service needs.

These include:

- Copying statements.

- Filling out applications, new account forms, IRA applications, etc.

- Changing titles into the client's living trust.

- Change of dealer forms.

- Trustee to trustee transfers.

- Direct rollover forms and status of the IRA transfers.

- Correcting spelling of clients' names.

- Change of address.

- Letters of transmittal.

- Waiting for the clients to write out their check. (This often takes the longest time.)

- Calculation of basis of investments.

- Booking appointments.

STEP NINE: Delegate work using a Dictaphone.

A Dictaphone is an underused tool that saves you the time of writing out memos, letters and reports by hand. It takes eight times longer to write it down then it does to say it! If you are serious about working efficiently, you will give your assistant at least one tape every day!

STEP TEN: Delegate accounting to an accountant.

Many advisors do their own accounting or bookkeeping. It is very inexpensive to hire an outside professional who has the software packages and expertise to do it in a much faster, more economical manner. In addition to this, many advisors rank this as one of the lowest priorities and often never get around to even knowing what their bottom line is until after the end of the year! You should have your financial statements prepared at least quarterly and therefore an outside accountant is usually your best bet.

STEP ELEVEN: Keep your staff happy.

This is a very important final step to make the delegation of tasks continue to run smoothly. You've taken the time to carefully hire and train your staff; now don't forget to acknowledge their competence. Assistants are the lifeblood of your office, the communication link to your clients and prospects, and one of the major success factors in your business. If you make sure that your assistants know that you understand their importance, they will most likely act with even more professionalism and assist you even better. Frustrated sales assistants cost you money, so it is worth your effort to recognize and reward them for a job well done. (Rewards do not have to be monetary–often a day off, a gift or an award will work just as well.) Let assistants know when they have helped you reach a goal, and in turn help them reach their own goals by encouraging them to obtain additional licenses, take courses or attend seminars that will help their professional growth. With this being said, the hard truth is that sometimes there is no competence to reward or acknowledge. If you have made a mistake and hired someone who turns out to be incompetent, the best thing you can do for your business is cut your losses and replace that person with someone who is both willing and able to help you meet your goals.

5 Star Tip

Train your staff. To maximize your assistant's help, you must specifically put down on paper what you expect your assistant to do.

Make sure that each of your assistants has a duties list.

Summary

As you probably realize, these are only 10 of many keys to being a successful financial planner. We have worked with thousands of advisors over the years in our **2-Day Financial Advisor Boot Camps**, through our website **www.MDPRODUCER.com** and in our **Exclusive Coaching Group**, not to mention those we've talked to at our many speaking engagements around the country. It is from this experience and the information we have gathered from all those Financial Advisors that we were able to choose these 10 things as the ones that have had the most impact on the practices of so many advisors.

As you also probably realize after reading this book, many of these keys to success overlap. For example, the issue of having a niche and becoming a specialist certainly overlap. Your unique selling proposal and marketing plan overlap in some areas, and are both also key elements of your business plan. In addition to this, your ability to meet with enough qualified prospects and clients will vary depending on your ability to delegate less important tasks and on your marketing results as well.

Because these 10 areas are so important to your success and so interconnected, we believe it is essential to constantly review your existing operation to determine whether or not anything can be improved. When an advisor feels there is no way to improve the situation that is usually their first mistake! If you are not continually upgrading your services, your systems and your ways of doing business, you are probably not keeping up with all of the changes and technological advances that are available today.

Finally, we both want to wish you the best of luck with your practice. We hope you will implement many, if not all, of the tips and strategies outlined in this book. Please feel free to visit our website at **www.MDPRODUCER.com**, where much more information is available to our members. You can also contact us through the website - we welcome your questions or comments about this the book and its impact on your practice!

Unfortunately, many of you reading this book may have thought that these were good ideas, but you will not make any changes! This, unfortunately, is the art of procrastination!

Think about it.

Have any of you every recommended some obvious changes to your client's financial picture, yet the client never took any course of action?

Weren't you frustrated?

Especially if it was something that was very easy to do and they still would not make a change!

Well, unfortunately, even some of the financial advisors that we talk to still never make any changes. That is why one of the most important things to remember is:

Advice without implementation is worthless!

We can only help you with giving advice. However, you have to take the next step and implement some of these ideas if you are to make a change in your life.

We all know what the definition of insanity is — attempting to do the same thing over and over, the exact same way, but expecting to get different results! If you don't make any changes, how will your results differ?

Let us help you! If you even take three of these ideas and implement them in your practice, you will see significant changes almost immediately.

Let us know your feedback, questions, or comments. We look forward to hopefully seeing you soon at one of our presentations!

Yours truly,

Ken Unger and Thomas Gau

Ken Unger
President, Million Dollar Producer

Ken Unger is a seasoned and respected educator and trainer known throughout the financial industry for his knowledge, enthusiasm and high energy level. With over twenty years of experience, Ken is recognized by financial advisors nationwide for sharing efficient practice management strategies and effective sales and marketing ideas.

As President of Million Dollar Producer, Ken creates training materials and conducts training sessions for mid to high-level financial advisors. He is often featured and quoted in the financial media and press. Ken is currently a writer for *MorningStar Advisor* and has been quoted in various periodicals, including *The Wall Street Journal*. He has appeared on numerous financial television and radio shows.

Ken is continually sought after to motivate and educate, and has been a featured, keynote or guest speaker at several hundred industry meetings and conferences. He has held over 1,000 client seminars and has provided insight and direction to those in the highest levels of the financial planning industry. Ken is a graduate of Cornell University.

If you are interested in helping your Reps' production take a quantum leap, or want to maximize their efficiency, then Ken Unger is available as a speaker for your next conference or meeting.

Thomas B. Gau, CPA, CFP
CEO & Founder, Million Dollar Producer

Tom Gau is a financial planner, tax authority, speaker, eduacator, and producer. As an active, in-the-trenches Financial Planner, Tom produces over $3,000,000 a year in commissions and fees...*working only two weeks a month!* He has been in the financial services arena for over 20 years and has his BS, MBA, and CPA degrees.

Tom has earned many accolades and honors. He was selected as one of the "Top 200 Financial Advisors" in the U.S. by *Worth* magazine and is profiled in the industry best-seller *The Winner's Circle: How 30 Financial Advisors Became the Best in the Business* and the nationwide best-seller *The Tipping Point*.

Tom is recognized as a uniquely knowledgeable and motivational speaker on topics relating to tax, financial and retirement planning. He has authored many of the leading books on the IRA distribution rules and their tax consequences. Tom has been repeatedly quoted in magazines such as *Money*, *The Robb Report*, *Kiplinger's Personal Finance*, *Investment Advisor*, *Financial Advisor*, *Mutual Fund*, *The Wall Street Journal*, the *Los Angeles Times* and other prestigious publications.

Most importantly, Tom has found out that the key to success is not what you do, but *how* you do it ⸺ that the only difference between a big producer and one just stuck on a "plateau" is the systems that the planner uses day in and day out. He has shared his proven systems with thousands of financial professionals who have also experienced spectacular results. Tom enjoys teaching and training other Financial Advisors, explaining those systems and how to best implement them.

Resources Available From
<u>Million Dollar Producer</u>

If you found this book helpful, please take a moment to review some of the other products and services offered to Financial Advisors by Million Dollar Producer.

Our company's focus is on **not just what to do, but <u>how</u> to do it.** We do this by offering you systems, strategies, and tools that have been tested by Tom Gau himself in his practice and found to be efficient, effective and most importantly, monetarily rewarding! Our other products include our:

- **<u>www.MDPRODUCER.com</u> website**
- **Five Star Performance Series Training Programs**
- **Complete Client Seminar Packages**
- **2-Day Financial Advisor Boot Camp**
- **Exclusive Coaching Group**

Membership to our website
www.MDPRODUCER.com

You have surely heard the saying "the cobbler's kids never have any shoes". Unfortunately, this often applies to Financial Advisors. Are you one of the majority of advisors who concentrate so much on helping others plan for financial independence that you forget to do so for yourself? If so, this website was developed just for you!

Tom Gau has found the keys to success in financial planning. Instead of keeping them to himself, he is anxious to share them with you so that you too might bring your business to the heights you've dreamed of. It is possible to not only boost your production, but also work less, leaving you more time to enjoy your life. You can't do this unless you make changes. Our definition of insanity is doing the same thing over and over and expecting to get different results!

There are many barriers to becoming more successful, and this website specifically addresses those listed below, along with many others. Do any of these sound familiar to you?

- I need systems badly.
- I'm afraid I don't know everything.
- I don't deserve this.
- I don't have a fully defined niche.
- I'm doing everything for everyone.
- I don't have a business plan.
- I have too many clients and struggle to handle them.
- I'm on a plateau and can't seem to get to the next level.
- I've never had formal training on how to run my office.
- I'm a great producer but a terrible manager.
- I don't know how to manage my time efficiently.
- I don't know how to upgrade my practice.
- I don't have an effective marketing plan.

- I have trouble differentiating myself from my competition.
- I'm having trouble competing with the Internet.
- My closing rate is not as good as I would like it to be.

Are you skeptical that this website can offer you things you don't already know? Consider this: We know that you will be able to extract from this website *at the very least* one or two ways to;

1. Attract more suitable clients,
2. Increase your production with existing clients, or
3. Free up more of your time for family or recreation.

If you are able to do even one of those things, your membership will pay for itself.

Subscribers to *Golf Digest* don't expect that every article will dramatically improve their games. In the same way, especially if you're already a successful financial planner, you may find that not every section of the website will teach you something new. However, if your membership leads to only a couple of new clients or a few more hours to yourself, isn't that worth many times your investment?

This website is updated regularly and Members can also e-mail specific practice management questions to Tom Gau or Ken Unger, which are answered.

If you are interested in learning more about the **Million Dollar Producer** website, please visit us at **www.MDPRODUCER.com** or call us toll free at **(866) 866-0472.**

Five Star Performance Series Training Packages

Million Dollar Producer offers several proven training materials designed to help you improve your practice management and/or client interview skills. These are available on DVDs, with full instructions on exactly how to implement all strategies and recommendations. Some modules are accompanied by a workbook that allows the viewer to not only follow the presentation, but also learn **how** to use the information!

Our Five Star Performance Series of training topics include;

- **How to Master the Initial Client Interview**

- **How to Hold Successful Closing Meetings**

- **How to Double Your Production While Working Less**

- **How to Add Value for Your Clients in a Difficult Market**

For more information about our **Five Star Performance Series Training** products, visit the products section of **www.MDPRODUCER.com** or call **866-866-0472**.

Complete Client Seminar Packages

Are you looking to hold seminars that are proven but different from those already being held in your community? Are you tired of purchasing systems that don't work? Do you want a seminar written and held by a multi-million dollar producer? Try using one of the seminars Tom Gau is currently using in his practice with great success. Topics available include:

- **The Complete Retirement Seminar**
- **The Complete Inherited IRA Seminar**
- **Tax Law Seminar**
- **What Seniors Should Do In a Volatile Stock Market**
- **NASD-approved Product Breakfast Seminar**

Tom Gau and many other advisors have had incredible results with these exact seminars, and you can, too! In these packages, Tom shares with you every single thing he does to set up the seminar, market it, present it and then get the attendees into his office.

All seminar packages include:

- A Power Point presentation or slides,
- An ad and a flyer, and
- A video or CD of Tom Gau presenting the seminar.

Packages may also include a written script, a seminar setup checklist, a response form, sample handout packages for attendees including an evaluation form, instructions on how to conduct a successful seminar, sample certificate for a free consultation to be given to all attendees, plus all other ingredients you need to successfully address a lucrative group of prospects. Please refer to the Products section of our website, **www.MDPRODUCER.com**, for specific information about each package.

If you're not sure whether the whole seminar package is right for you, you can purchase just the 2-hour video of Tom Gau presenting the seminar. Learn from his presentation techniques and use this video as an invaluable training tool! Apply Tom Gau's unique approach to make both your seminar presentations and your face-to-face meetings even more effective (generate more appointments and increase your closing ratio).

If you are interested in learning more about our proven Client Seminar Packages, please visit the product section of **www.MDPRODUCER.com** or call us toll free at **(866) 866-0472.**

<u>Coaching and Training Sessions</u>

Tom Gau and Ken Unger have presented to and/or trained over 100,000 financial advisors and are among the most sought after speakers in the financial planning industry. *The New York Times'* best-seller *The Tipping Point* lists **Tom Gau** as a marketing and training guru, and he's featured in the industry's best-seller *The Winner's Circle: How Thirty Financial Advisors Became the Best in the Business.*

If you would like these two trainers to take your production to the highest levels possible, or if you are interested in some of the most efficient systems for Financial Advisors, then you can attend Million Dollar Producer's **2-Day Financial Advisor Boot Camp** or enroll in their **Exclusive Coaching Program**.

2-Day Financial Advisor Boot Camp

This 2-Day Financial Advisor Boot Camp will sharpen every aspect of your financial planning practice and approach. It will review the most effective methods of marketing, client acquisition and retention, financial planning, time management, successful client interview techniques, referral generation, closing techniques and much more. You will leave this session armed with the following:

- Immediate changes you can make to increase production while working less.
- Proven techniques to increase your assets under management.
- The secrets of maximizing referral generation.
- Ways to consistently get in front of more qualified, high-net-worth prospects.
- Time-tested tips for retaining existing clients.
- Strategies for holding the most effective meetings with prospects and clients.
- Systems to increase your efficiency in all aspects of your business.
- Organizational techniques to maximize the productivity of your entire office.
- A full package of handouts, including helpful checklists.

If you're still not sure this is right for you, then visit our website to read what some of the more than 20,000 Financial Advisors who have already benefited from our **2-Day Financial Advisor Boot Camp** have to say.

Here are two examples:

"They (Tom and Ken) provided me with strong and effective systems and strategies. After implementing these strategies, my production tripled in less than 18 months! Now, I consistently qualify as one of the top producers in my firm. Their sessions are a must for any successful producer." -S.E., Edgewater, MD

"I thought it was a great session! I would've paid a lot more for it! My production increased significantly after using the information given in just the first 30 minutes!" -B.A., Sacramento, CA

If you are interested in learning more about the **2-Day Financial Advisor Boot Camp**, please call Million Dollar Producer toll free at **(866) 866-0472.**

Exclusive Coaching Program

This Exclusive program is for a limited number of Financial Advisors who are looking for a way to break through to the highest levels of production and efficiency. Tom Gau and Ken Unger will personally coach you on how to increase your production, maximize your efficiency, free up more time for family or recreation, keep all your existing clients satisfied, and strengthen your practice in general. Exclusive Coaching Group Advisors will participate in;

- **3 two-day meetings,**
- **6 conference calls, and**
- **4 one-on-one personal coaching sessions (30 minutes each)**

Some of the topics covered in the Exclusive Coaching Program include;

- Drafting your custom marketing and business plan
- Proven marketing techniques
- Seminar marketing
- Holding successful quarterly and annual client review sessions
- Perfecting your initial client interview
- Setting the proper goals for your business
- Attracting high-net-worth clients
- Closing prospective clients
- Efficient time management techniques

- Creating and implementing your annual business plan
- Growing your practice during difficult times
- Offering a "can't miss" package of services
- Tax and estate planning (*not preparation*) strategies
- Wealth transfer techniques
- Increasing your production
- Hiring efficient and effective staff
- Expanding your business and your office personnel
- What and how to delegate
- How to best use a Junior Representative
- Keys to office and staff management
- Establishing a practice that has future value

But remember, this is a personal coaching experience. You can work on the areas *you* need to work on. Tom Gau and Ken Unger commit their energy, talent and passion to making this a very rewarding experience for you. Their goal is to make the lives of their coaching students easier, better and more rewarding.

"As a Million Dollar Producer, I think this session is a no-brainer and a must for high level practitioners. I would have easily paid a multiple of the tuition for this information. Thank you Tom and Ken for being my coach." -M.P., Illinois.

If you are interested in learning more about the **Exclusive Coaching Program**, please call Million Dollar Producer toll free at **(866) 866-0472.**

iy
breads
are taxable does it mean
Bra
tax
shelter